SECRET OF RIGHT ACTIVITY

SECRET OF RIGHT ACTIVITY

SWAMI PARAMANANDA

GYAN

Published by

Gyan Publishing House
5, Ansari Road
Daryaganj, New Delhi-110002
Phone: 011-47034999, 9811692060
E-mail: books@gyanbooks.com

Distribution Network
gyanbooks.com
India, USA, Canada, UK, Australia

ISBN: 978-93-64330-695 (PB)

First Published, 1923

2nd Impression 2024

Printed at: Gyan Press, Delhi.

SECRET OF RIGHT ACTIVITY
Author: SWAMI PARAMANANDA

Practical Series No. 6

Secret of Right Activity

Secret of Right Activity

BY

SWAMI PARAMANANDA

AUTHOR OF "SOUL'S SECRET DOOR," "THE VIGIL," "REINCARNATION AND IMMORTALITY," "THE WAY OF PEACE AND BLESSEDNESS," "CREATIVE POWER OF SILENCE," "EMERSON AND VEDANTA," ETC.

THIRD EDITION
REVISED AND ENLARGED

Published by
THE VEDANTA CENTRE, Boston, Mass.

ANANDA ASHRAMA
La Crescenta, Los Angeles Co., Calif.

Reprinted from the Vedanta Monthly
"THE MESSAGE OF THE EAST"

PRINTED IN U.S.A.

CONTENTS

I.

SECRET OF RIGHT ACTION

Righteousness is the accordance of actions with what is right. In all things success depends on previous preparation; without such preparation there is failure. —*Confucius.*

Do not waste your life in doubts and fears; spend yourself on the work before you, well assured that the right performance of this hour's duties will be the preparation for the hours or ages to follow.—*Benjamin Franklin.*

THE secret of right action in reality is not a secret. It does not lie in any formula that we repeat. There is no magic by means of which we can follow the path of idleness and yet make our life productive. No! The secret lies in our own motives, in our power of application. It is not the strong physical vehicle which makes the productive human being; it is skillfulness in action, knowing how to adjust ourselves quickly, how to perform a task with the least expenditure of energy. This is what gives immediate success.

There are some people who talk little and accomplish more, while others talk much and accomplish nothing. Though a man may speak very glibly on religion, on the great ideals of love, service and brotherhood, that does not make him religious. But if he is "a doer of the law," as Christ said, even in a small measure; if he knows how to direct his life and its forces, he will not only be religious, he will be a better, stronger human being and his influence will reach others. This is what I call practical religion—a religion productive of good, of men and women of an inspiring type; not the morbid religion which merely clings to dogma. Not that!

One of the most interesting studies in life is to note how our false concept can distort even a holy example, so that it no longer bears any resemblance to the original idea. For instance, the average man looks upon the world of religion as entirely apart from active life. He thinks that in order to become religious one must abandon worldly activities and assume a mournful, repentant attitude. This is not a true conception of religion. What good will even the loftiest ideal do us or our fellow-men, if we do not live it and bring it to fruition? Unless it gives us something definite and dynamic it might just as well not exist for us. The whole purpose of religion and philosophy is to give us that which is inspiring, elevating and constructive. Merely going to church or professing a creed, whether it be Christianity or Buddhism or any "ism", is not active religion. It is not practical religion. It is a mockery. It is degradation for the soul of the individual and for the soul of the race. It can only produce hypocrites and fanatics.

True religion we carry into our outer activities; we make it alive, alert, productive. If a person does nothing and gives nothing for the benefit of his fellows, how do we know he is religious? Merely upholding a theory has no value. If we have high ideals we must express them in our lives. This problem confronts us all. Whether we are laymen or in the religious life makes no difference whatsoever. We are living souls in contact with other living souls; we have to be active. These are the ideals of Karma Yoga, the great Indian system of right action. It proclaims that religion is not only for the man who is inactive. On the contrary it holds that the man who is active and energetic, who is constantly doing something in the world, has just as much right to enter the kingdom of heaven as the hermit without duties and without obligations. It pays great tribute to the people who live in the world and keep their ideal intact. They are the heroes.

There is no one who can claim that he does not need to take part in active life. Whether we spend our days at home or go out daily, we must be doing something for our self-preservation. A man who does nothing, his mind and his physical vehicle quickly deteriorate. He becomes dead although carrying on an existence. One who is so convinced of his own principles that he is indifferent to what others say, and who is willing to give himself to his task, that man will accomplish his purpose. Great artists know this, also scientists, though perhaps unconsciously. They plunge into their work.

There are moments when we forget our environment, forget everything but the one thing that we are doing, and those are the supreme moments of our life. They make it possible for us to attain success. How does the average person work? He works with a sense of weight and drudgery or else with feverish intensity. Either will break him. One who works with indifference, how can he accomplish anything? His heart is not in it. His mind, his soul, his energies are all divided. If our heart is not in our task, we shall resemble laborers who have no real interest in what they are doing; they only pretend. If they break things they do not care; they merely want their wage. Such work can never bring satisfaction to us or to any one and we learn nothing from it. When the aim is low it can only produce something very small and unsatisfying. On the other hand, a person who is driven by the fever of a selfish motive, who works with nervous excitement, how long will he last? Sooner or later he will break his machine.

What we need is the understanding spirit, the love element. By that I mean we must learn to love the task we are performing. Any machine which does not receive sufficient lubrication will break very quickly, and it is the element of understanding, of love, which keeps our human machine well-oiled. No one can do his work properly unless he has feeling. A person with cut and dried attitude may try to do his duty, but he will not be really productive. Many charitable organizations are like that. They are excellent institutions, but they seem to be untouched by human feeling. It is not intended for human beings to destroy the finer part of their life and become like machines. We may direct a machine, we may use it, but we must have intelligence and feeling in abundance. It is not an arduous task to put these ideas and ideals into practice. What we do now with small selfish mind, we can do just as well with idealistic motive. It will refresh us. Instead of feeling crushed and broken down by our work, we shall be filled with energy, we shall have greater inspiration.

We have spoken of master artists, musicians and scientists; how through concentration and one-pointed love for their art, they attain their ideal. An ordinary person, when he undertakes anything, at once begins to think of the money he is going to get out of it, or of some other return. It stands to reason that he cannot fill his mind with these calculations and not weaken it for the task in hand. The logic is plain. Instead of doing his work with the wholeness of his being, he is dividing himself into many parts; he is thinking of the non-essentials. Naturally his return will be small. He has scattered his forces, thereby wasting his time. Work done in this way, half-heartedly, with distracted mind, must be done badly and often has to be done over again. Poor laborers turn out this sort of work, or sometimes shrewd people who think it will pass unnoticed. But there are others more shrewd and they find it out. This not only means lost labor, but it has a very demoralizing effect upon the laborer.

Action and reaction are constantly taking place in this world. No one can escape them. We may declare that we are going to have in our life only happiness and beauty, that we will have riches and not poverty. But the pairs of opposites are always playing back and forth. We cannot have happiness without unhappiness. We cannot have light without darkness. What is the remedy? It is given in the Gita: "To work alone thou hast the right, but never to the fruits thereof." The man who is a slave to his passions, who is bound by small ideas of gain and loss, must suffer from reaction.

Suppose we scheme and plan and then

something goes wrong? We not only lose that which we have set our heart upon, but we no longer have the will or inclination to try again. The man of discerning mind, however, who understands the secret and is not attached to results, rises above failure. He does better the next time and still better, till he finally succeeds. He gives no thought to the fruit of his effort. The fruit will come when we are deserving of it, and we make ourselves deserving by learning to throw our entire being into our acts. This is what makes us dynamic. Leave the fruit for the time being. Do not be afraid that some one else will take it from you. No one can. What is your rightful heritage will be yours.

If it is a fact that you do not want to lose anything, physically, mentally, morally or spiritually, then do not play the losing game. Never think anything too small to do. The truly great do not differentiate between big tasks and little. Their keenness, their power of appreciation, their desire to do well what they do, makes them forget that a task is little. This is the true sign of greatness. Men of vision, men of genius, never feel that any work is beneath them. There is nothing beneath us and nothing beyond us. That should be our attitude.

By doing small tasks whole-heartedly, with concentration and skillfulness, we evolve within ourselves a power which will enable us later on to perform some great task which now seems like a mountain, inaccessible and unobtainable. It will melt away before us when we know the secret, and this power of single-hearted devotion is the secret. It is a gift, an inspiration, subtle and noiseless. We cannot force it upon another mind. Each soul must evolve it. That which we evolve within saturates our whole life. We may not be regarded as religious by our community, but that makes no difference. We carry a sustaining influence. When an emergency arises, we know how to adjust ourselves quickly. We possess the power to do our work, no matter what its nature, and come out unsullied and unspoiled.

Do not imagine, therefore, that religion means retiring from the world. That idea brought corruption among the great schools of philosophy and religion in ancient time. Disciples began to think that the religious life meant simply withdrawing and meditating. Meditation—true meditation—is a very active thing. It means first seeing clearly, then putting into practice what we see. Love is an abstract ideal if we lay it to one side, but the act of loving service, filling the heart with love and expressing it through our life, brings a dynamic return. Think what a tremendous benefit it would be to the world, if all men who believed in Christ and His message of love would practise this love even in small measure. What a mighty thing it would be if the five hundred million people who profess Buddhism would follow the wonderful example of their compassionate teacher Gautama Buddha and practise non-killing,—not merely refraining from partaking of animal food, but never harming another by a hateful thought, actually practising non-injury in thought, word and deed. What an atmosphere would be created in this world! And that is what the world needs to-day.

The superiority of any religion or philosophy lies in its practical life and not in its theories or dogmas. Religions are not high or low because of these. Each religion has one supreme pinnacle, but it is when we touch practical living that we bring to fruition all that these great ideals stand for. We go on with a sense of consecration, a sense of higher duty. The nature of our work does not matter. It is not high office that ennobles a man, but his motive. We need not boast because of any position that we hold, or feel degraded because of lack of opportunities. Opportunities will come when we have proved our fitness. That is the law of compensation.

There is an Indian parable of a rich man who employed two servants, one, a talker, clever and convincing; the other, not so skilled in words, but industrious, always busy in the orchard. One day the rich man came to visit the garden. The clever, shrewd servant began to praise his master's person, flattering him, telling him how beautiful were his hands and face and everything pertaining to his personality. The other servant said nothing; he went and gathered all the fruits and flowers that he had produced through his silent labor and placed them before his master. With which do you suppose the master was pleased?

It is not the talker, the noisy, aggressive type of human being who produces the most or who brings the greatest amount of blessing. It is the quiet, concentrated worker. Although he asks nothing, he receives everything. Whether we care for the fruit or not, it will come to us when we deserve it. Let us carry this in our mind, in our consciousness. It will ennoble us; it will heal our wounds when we are disappointed. We are placed here by a divine hand. To disconnect ourselves from that, to feel and think that we are isolated and unprotected, existing merely for our own self-gratification, is the greatest tragedy that can befall us. To restore ourselves to that One is to rid the soul of selfish desires.

Let us have a great ideal, an ideal that will startle us with its greatness. That is the only kind of an ideal to hold before our mind's eye and to work for. Little by little our imperfections and difficulties will vanish and instead of regarding life as a drudgery, instead of shrinking from it, we shall bless this life which offers so many opportunities. We shall find joy even in the little daily tasks and where-ever we are placed we shall know happiness.

II.

THE RELIGION OF WORK

If by study, enquiry or thought, we have learned the truth, we should then put it into practice in both our speech and action. Let what we say be true and what we do discreet. Regulate the emotions, and suppress anger and selfish desires. Shake off evil and cling to good. Discovering our faults, let us not hesitate to correct them. Towards others let us be considerate. All this is the way of true action. . . . Without putting what we have learned into practice, it bears no fruit.—*Kaibara Ekken, Japanese Sage.*

Righteousness can be practised only when we have freed our mind from passions of egotism. Perfect peace can dwell only where all vanity has disappeared.—*Buddha.*

TRUE religion teaches us how to do well all that we undertake, so that we may prove ourselves worthy servants of the Lord, faithful in our present position before being promoted to something greater. The greatest Truth-seers the world has ever produced were men of wonderful activity. They were equally mighty and efficient on all planes. The difference between the spiritually awakened man and the ordinary type of worker lies, not in the amount of his activity, but in its quality and motive power. The spiritual man works with understanding and skill, therefore he accomplishes most with least effort; while the ordinary worker wastes much of his energy through ignorance of the higher laws. In both cases we find the same manifestation of activity. The ordinary man, however, being too limited and self-centred to grasp anything far-reaching, works for small ends and reaps small results; while the spiritually-minded man, whose work is free from all ulterior motive, works for large ends and achieves lasting results.

But is there any difference in the nature of work? Is there any kind of activity which is absolutely free from evil? No; there is no work which is absolutely good or absolutely bad. It is our motive in the work which determines its worth. We know that there is within us a pent-up energy which is constantly finding its outlet through thought, words and actions. We can use this energy for our best happiness and upliftment; or we can misuse it and cause our own ruin. It can manifest itself in the form of anger or hatred, which will bring disastrous results; also it can manifest itself in the form of goodness, unselfish love, charity and service. It is the same energy expressing itself in different ways according to our tendency.

One who falls back or becomes degraded, has allowed his force to drag him down; and through the proper use of it the same man has the power to uplift himself. Therefore the sages teach us never to condemn or look down upon any one, but always to speak words of encouragement and show the way by which others may discover the secret of right activity and raise themselves. Since by our nature we must all be constantly active, what we need is to learn to direct our forces through right channels and avoid painful reactions.

The aim of Karma Yoga is to teach us how by the least expenditure of effort we can accomplish most. Now what should be the nature of our work when we follow this path? Religious teachers often tell us that in order to be spiritual we must become contemplative; but we are honest when we say that we have no time to spend in that way; so we give up all religious hope and effort, because these teachers are unable to offer us something else which would be as helpful as contemplation. Understanding this, the ancient Aryans did not prescribe just one particular method of religious training. They developed different methods suited to the varying conditions and temperaments of different individuals. In this way no one has to go contrary to his nature. These paths are four in number, with numerous sub-divisions, which provide for all phases of human development and give to each an equal opportunity to realize the truth. They are the path of work, the path of devotion, the path of self-control and the path of philosophy or wisdom.

The first path, Karma Yoga, may be called the religion of work. It is particularly intended for men and women in active life. To follow it one need not necessarily believe in any religious creed. There are workers who do not even believe in a personal God, but they work unselfishly and their God is the God of service. Whatever they do, therein God dwells. In their office, in their home, in all their activities they carry with them the ideal of service. And this is one of the great methods taught by the Seers, and one which among the ancient Aryans was practised by the busiest men we can imagine—by kings and emperors, soldiers and artisans. They followed this path and attained the same unfoldment as those who chose the contemplative life or the path of renunciation.

We must all work incessantly. What we need is the right motive. We can work in a way which will bring us the choicest blessings, and also the same work, done with a different spirit, will bring us bondage. The main secret is to learn to work without attachment. Work like a master and not as a slave. Work for work's sake; love for love's sake. We have a notion that unless we are ambitious and eager for the fruits of our work, we shall not accomplish anything; or that unless we have strong attachment for a person, we cannot do so well for that person. But this is not true. Attachment is not love. Attachment makes us demand, while love unfolds the capacity for giving. If we really love the art of our work, we shall be more interested in how well we can do it than in how much we are going to gain from it. Also, if we have true love for any one, we shall be more concerned for his joy and blessing than for our own gratification. When we are merely attached to the fruits of our work and do not get the result we desire, we become discouraged and give up easily; but when we work out of love for the work itself, no matter how many times we fail to get the desired result, we keep on. This constant concern for gain and loss hampers our free action and impedes our spiritual progress.

"To work we have the right, not to the fruits thereof," this is the motto of all true workers. How often we misunderstand this supreme teaching of the Bhagavad Gita, thinking it impossible to work without setting our heart on the result. But it does not mean that we have to forfeit all the blessings that we earn; it only teaches us how we can avoid unpleasant reactions. Every action must be followed by a reaction, as every cause is followed by an effect. Like a small boat on the high seas, so do we rise and fall with every wave of action and reaction so long as we work with attachment. All our pleasure and pain, smiles and tears, are wholly the reactions of our own actions. No matter how much we may like to have only the pleasure-giving reactions, it is impossible to get the one without the other. Recognizing this fact, wise men try to rise above this shifting plane of duality and to work independently, without regard for the results that may come. This brings tranquillity and steadfastness in work.

Great Souls, like Jesus the Christ,

Buddha and other divine Manifestations, have proved this. Work for work's sake was the main principle in their character and in their life. They worked without seeking personal gain or tangible immediate results. How few welcomed them when they brought the message of Truth! How much antagonism they met! And yet they went on steadily, because they did it all through love, without any ulterior motive. If you are helping a person, do not expect that person to be grateful to you. Do not always trade in your love. Nobody can be a true worker without disinterested love in his heart. It is the oil which makes the machine of life run smoothly; and unless we have genuine love, we suffer.

We know from our own experience that whenever we love a person, no matter how tired we are, we like to do for him with our own hands. We do not trust any substitute to serve that one whom we love most truly; and our service makes us forget for the time being that we are tired. The physical constitution is largely dependent on the mind and mind is dependent on the thought-force; hence when our thought is connected with some noble motive, it brings us refreshment. A nervous breakdown does not come because of the work we do in life. If we have proper understanding, we do not have to suffer from any breakdown. It is the lack of an ideal, the lack of consecration which wears us out; and those who work thoughtfully gradually realize this.

The ideal Karma Yogis, those who follow the path of work, always surrender the fruits of their labor unto God, realizing Him as the doer; therefore they are never attached. When the reaction of suffering comes, they do not identify themselves with it; and when pleasure comes, they are not carried away by it. If they are praised, they do not grow egotistical, believing that they are the doers; neither when they are blamed do they succumb to it, thinking that they are responsible. You may say that this will make us irresponsible. No, not so. It will lead us to the Christ-like state, "Not my will, but Thine"; and only when it brings us to that attitude shall we know how to act. Before that, although we may be working and trying to grow, we simply create impediments along our way by our thoughts and actions.

As long as we are unselfish, so long we are the gainers; but whenever we bring the thought of self, we suffer, because we demand. We demand from the person we love; and if we do not get what we demand, we naturally suffer from reaction. Therefore the path of work teaches us how to do for others without thought of return. It is freedom from all dependence in action which brings us real peace and rest.

Karma Yoga says that each is great in his own place. One is living the life of a householder. He need not think he is inferior to one who leads the life of renunciation. We all create, we all have an equal share in this universe; so we must never have the attitude that any one place or task in life is inferior; neither should we think that God cannot be attained by living in the world and doing our duties there. On the contrary, true performance of duty will bring us great spiritual results.

Thus we see that the different paths which men follow, according to their conviction, all lead to the same ultimate goal of Truth. A very beautiful illustration is given in one of our Scriptures to show that no matter where a man is placed, he can become religious and get inspiration through faithfully fulfilling his duties. There was once a monk who lived the life of contemplation. After several years of practice he was sitting under a tree one day, when he was disturbed by the falling of some leaves on his head and he found that two birds in quarrelling had caused them to drop. This irritated him so much that a flash of light came from his eyes and destroyed the birds. We can always develop so-called miraculous power if we live a steady life, and the monk had gained this power through his practice of austerity. Seeing what he was able to do, he grew conceited and thought he had attained the highest.

He went to a neighboring village for his alms, knocking at the door of a householder. The lady of the house was nursing her sick husband and could not come at once, so she asked him to wait. The monk, remembering the birds, thought with irritation: "How dare she keep me waiting?" The woman at once replied: "Here is neither crow nor crane." Surprised, he asked her: "How did you know my thoughts?" She said: "My son, I have never practised any Yoga. Merely by the faithful performance of my duties have I gained this clear sight." The ascetic then bowed down before her and begged to be taught by her; but the lady told him to go to a butcher who lived in a certain village and who would explain to him more about Truth.

He found the butcher engaged in his work of cutting and selling meat. When he had attended to all his duties—closing his stall, washing and feeding his aged parents—he came to the ascetic and inquired what service he could render him. The ascetic then asked him many questions regarding the soul, its relation to

God, and other difficult problems, to which the butcher replied in a simple manner; and the illumined words which he spoke are known as the Vyadha-Gita or "The Song of the Butcher." After listening to him, the ascetic asked: "Why, with all this wonderful wisdom, do you follow such an unclean trade?" He replied: "My son there is nothing unclean in life. No duty is impure or low. It all depends upon our own mental attitude. The Lord has placed me in this position, I have tried to do my duty faithfully and without attachment, and all that I have gained has come through that."

For a true worker there is nothing unholy, there is nothing mean or low. Whatever his work, he may bring the choicest blessings through it, if he has the right spirit; and this is what we have to learn. We must learn to live in the world, as Sri Krishna teaches in the Bhagavad Gita, like a lotus leaf, which grows in water but is never wet by the water. The entire universe is before us. It creates bondage for those who do not know how to use it; but it gives freedom, peace and blessing to those who know how. The great Karma Yogis say to us: Live in this world freely. We are the children of God. All is given by Him. Do not be attached to material things. Have a broad view of life. Do not cling to things which are non-essential. Perform all work for the purification of your soul; not with the idea of earning a wage, but with some really noble motive.

We, direct descendants of the Almighty, should not waste our energy for petty selfish ends, but we should learn to work without ulterior motive. Work always bears fruit. Work always creates. It can create freedom or it can create bondage. Both ways are open before us

—the path which causes suffering and the path which leads to eternal happiness and peace. True sincere souls continue to work, but their work releases them from all bondage.

Our actions are nothing but the manifestation of our thoughts and therefore we must learn to think correctly. If our thoughts are spiritual, then our work necessarily will be so in accord with universal law that we can never do anything injurious to ourselves or to others. Those who constantly work with this spirit, knowing that they are instruments in the hands of God, come so near to Him that they can never go astray. Wherever we may be placed, let us not cut ourselves off from the higher Source. Let us not think that we are puny mortals. Let us not think that we have no work to do in the world. Rather let us believe that we have a great work, because we are children of God. We all have a distinct mission in life and we must carry out that mission through proper understanding and right action.

Thus the religion of work or Karma Yoga teaches us how we can consecrate every bit of our activity to the Supreme; how we can perform our duty with freedom and love, avoiding the beggarly attitude of expecting return or recognition. When the right understanding of the law dawns in our heart, then even the humblest forms of activity may become acts of worship and lead to the highest spiritual attainment. As the Lord declares in the Bhagavad-Gita: "He who worketh for Me alone, hath Me for his highest goal, who is devoted to Me, who is freed from attachment, and beareth enmity towards no creature, such a person attaineth unto Me."

III.
DUTY AND SERVICE

The path of duty lies in what is near, and men seek for it in what is remote. The work of duty lies in what is easy, and men seek for it in what is difficult.—*Mencius.*

When thou makest a dinner, call not thy friends, nor thy brethren, neither thy kinsmen, nor the rich neighbors, lest they also bid thee again, and a recompense be made thee. But when thou makest a feast, call the poor, the maimed, the lame, the blind, and thou shalt be blessed. —*Jesus the Christ.*

IS there any common standard of duty? In studying the ethical laws of various peoples, we are led to believe that there cannot be any universal objective standard; but there is a subjective principle which underlies the moral codes of all nations. The outward form of duty changes according to our position in life. It can never be defined therefore by any fixed set of rules. That which might be a duty in one condition would not be under other circumstances. All objective duty is determined by a man's relation to his external environment, hence it must necessarily remain relative; but subjective duty concerns only man himself and his character. It has to do, not with his action, but with his motive; with a principle, not with its mode of application; therefore there can be an abstract law common to all mankind. It may be summed up thus: "That which makes a man forget his own little self for others and leads him towards his Ideal is his highest duty."

It is not possible, however, to reach this abstract subjective ideal without first following the path of immediate outer duties. We must begin by fulfilling the obligations which are nearest to us. First we must perform our duty towards our family, our community, our country; then as our heart grows in understanding and sympathy, we are gradually able to do our share of good to all living beings. But we cannot realize this great ideal and undertake the larger tasks of life until we have proved ourselves by ably performing the small ones at our hand; and no matter how insignificant or unpleasant these may seem, they are the only ones for us. As it is said in the Bhagavad-Gita: "Better one's own duty, though devoid of merit, than the duty of another well-performed. Better is death in following one's own duty; the duty of another is full of danger." Why? Because nothing can be gained by undertaking an alien duty.

We must not forget that the purpose of life is evolution. All our present conditions and obligations are the result of our own past actions; and only as we meet them wisely, can we rise to higher conditions and be entrusted with greater responsibilities. We must show ourselves worthy in our present position, then when we have earned greater things they will be given to us. We may imagine that we could do better some other task than the one which stands before us; but if it were substituted for our present one, very soon we should find that we were not fitted for it.

In the preliminary stages of our spiritual development, we must faithfully pursue the path of duty prescribed by our life and conditions; then our nature will become so expanded that all feeling of compulsion will cease to exist and every task will seem to us a privilege. When in all our work we are actuated by love, not by a sense of obligation, then duty is transformed into service and we accomplish it spontaneously, just for the joy we find in doing it. A sense of duty most often implies limitation, because it springs from a feeling of obligation; but in service we give freely. There is no calculation, no thought of coercion.

The spirit of true service, however, never dawns in the heart without self-abnegation and non-attachment. If we would do for others, we must be willing to forget our own little self, our physical comforts, our individual happiness. Only as all our actions are based on the principle of working, not for results, but through love, do we learn to help others truly. A worthy lover of mankind is like a flower, which gives its fragrance whether we place it on our head or trample it under our feet. His nature is to give without any regard for his own personal gain or loss.

The story is told of a holy man in India who, going one day to a well to drink, found a scorpion struggling in the water. The sight touched his loving heart and lifting the poor creature from the well, he pressed it against his breast to warm and revive it. But no sooner had the scorpion regained its strength than it stung him. The saint placed it gently on the ground and in a moment it fell back into the well. Forgetting that it had done him any injury, again he rescued it and held it against his heart, but the scorpion stung him as before. Still a third time he drew it from the water and gave it the same loving care, wholly unmindful of the harm done to himself. He had reached a state of consciousness where he realized the ideal preached by Buddha and Christ of loving even his enemies, for all self-love had merged into the great love which embraces every living creature.

The first quickening in the spiritual life is marked by the awakening of feeling for others. As we read in the Gita: "He who looks upon pleasure and pain everywhere with the same regard as when it is applied to himself, that one is highest"; because this signifies the broadening of the whole nature. As long as our interests remain confined within the circle of our little self, all struggle for higher attainment is in vain. That is why all the ethical and spiritual teachings of the world unanimously proclaim the necessity of cultivating selflessness through the practice of charity and compassion.

When we serve for the sake of serving, when we love for the joy of loving, when we act without selfish motive, we become ideal characters. Those who are sincere, pure-hearted, true lovers of their fellow-men never hurt any one by thought, word or deed. According to the Vedic teaching: "Doing good to others is the only virtue, injuring another is the only vice." He who hurts no living creature by his thoughts, his words or his actions is indeed a saint and a true representative of religion, whether or not he ever enters a place of worship.

Every act of our life can be done in such a way as to uplift us or to drag us down. It is not what we do, but how we do it that determines the merit of each action. Therefore we must learn to live and work with humility, non-attachment, sympathy and selfless love. When all these are combined in our efforts to serve God and our fellow-beings, then alone we are serving truly. And such service is the highest aim of human life.

IV.

RIGHT THINKING AND RIGHT LIVING

All our dignity consists in thought. By this must we raise ourselves, not by space or duration which we cannot fill. Then let us make it our study to think well; for this is the starting-point of morals.—*Pascal.*

Men must be decided on what they will not do, then they are able to act with vigor in what they ought to do. —*Mencius.*

"EARNESTNESS is the path of immortality, thoughtlessness is the path of death. Those who are in earnest do not die, those who are thoughtless are as if dead already. If an earnest person has roused himself, if he is not forgetful, if his deeds are pure, if he acts with consideration, if he restrains himself and lives according to the Law, then his glory will increase." Such are the words of Buddha. It is thought which moulds our character. Of all factors it is the mightiest in shaping human life and destiny; and unless we pay proper attention to our thought, it is impossible to accomplish anything. A man may work, he may struggle to gain some end, but if he has not the right understanding, that is, if he has not awakened the faculty of right thinking, he is like a boatman who is pulling on his oars without having drawn up his anchor. The boat will not go forward. Similarly those who have not roused themselves from the slumber of ignorance, no matter what they may try to do, they will not succeed.

The power of right thinking must be awakened; that is the first step. We all think; but thought is of two kinds:—one kind is constructive, it uplifts man to great heights; the other is destructive, it degrades and instead of helping proves a great drawback. Yet the same mind is used for both. It is said in one of the Upanishads: "This mind is the cause of bondage and of liberation for all human beings. If attached to the world, it becomes bound; if freed from the world, that is liberty." How is it that the same mind can play such a double part? Because the mind can either go downward or it can go upward, whichever way we choose to direct it. It is ready to serve us and lead us onward; and if we neglect it, it will bind us and draw us back to the brute plane. Therefore we cannot afford to disregard this important factor; for right thought is the fly-wheel of this great machine of human life and unless it revolves properly, the machine can do nothing. It may even be destroyed; if we are not discriminative, we may make mistakes which will prove our ruin.

In the Upanishads this body has been compared to a chariot, the senses are the horses, the mind is the reins, the intellect is the driver, and the Self who dwells within is the Lord of the chariot. Unless the horses are well controlled and the reins firmly held, unless the driver is intelligent, the chariot may be thrown into the ditch and destroyed. But if the discriminative faculty is awake, that is, if the driver follows the path of right thinking, then he has perfect control over both horses and chariot.

There are people who appear to have complete control over their mind. What gives them this power? It comes from right thinking and right living, for right thinking and right living go together. Only the man who lives in the right way, whose thoughts do not betray him, whose mind and mouth are one, as Sri Ramakrishna has said, that is, whose inner thought and outer activity are in perfect harmony: he alone will be able to accomplish great things. No one can do great things unless he first thinks great things. Those who have ambitions and try to realize them by over-riding their fellow-beings can only attain ephemeral results. Right thinking means that we do not wish to hurt any one; we may want to progress, but not at the cost of another. There cannot be any selfish idea in it. We desire to grow only in order that our growth may prove a help to mankind. No one can really grow who thinks wholly of himself or even of those who stand closest to him.

Unless we take all mankind into consideration, our growth cannot be far-reaching; we cannot become great. That is the reason why the first principle of all religious teachers has been to hate no man, to conquer everything through love; because love is constructive. Even when we wish to create something great for ourselves, if we try to obtain it through hatred, we shall find that it crumbles very soon, because there is a destructive element in it. Those who seek to harm their fellowmen inevitably meet with punishment sooner or later. The law of this world makes them unhappy and they will be unhappy hereafter, for the hereafter is nothing but the resultant of what we do here. It is not enough to pray or work for our own happiness and peace; there cannot be any true happiness or peace unless it encircles others. All are related to us in spirit; and if we hate any one we are hating something which is part of ourselves. This realization of universal oneness in spirit destroys what we call evil.

Why is it that we think so much of earthly possessions, of wealth and prosperity, of all such things which begin and end with this life; while we scarcely give a thought to that which is lasting, to that which concerns our soul? Yet we pose as intelligent human beings. If any one among us tries to live a different kind of life and apply the Gospel of Truth given by the Illumined Ones, we think that that person is doing wrong. Is thinking of God and Truth wrong? Is serving a lofty ideal wrong? That is a superstition which we must remove from our heart if we would progress. All erroneous and weakening thoughts must be rooted out if we want to advance either physically or morally or spiritually. Too often such thoughts are put into our heads in childhood, that we must live in a certain way and not do anything different from those with whom we are associated. If all those about us were ideal characters, it might be right for us to follow in their footsteps. But our soul-hunger is for something else and we must gain that.

When we study the teaching of the Vedas, we find that it insists upon one thing,—being and becoming. Man must become; he must become one with Truth. How? He must first wake himself from the sleep of ignorance. He must acquire strength. A man who is weak cannot attain the Truth, therefore let him be strong. He must not think that he is a sinner, that he is born in sin and iniquity. On the contrary, he must feel imbued with the idea that he is a child of God; that although he may have made mistakes, yet there is hope for him because he is a child of God. Strengthening, lofty thought enables us to counteract the weakness which is so dominant in our nature at present. When our mind is fixed on a high ideal and we become imbued with it, then our actions will spontaneously express it. Now we are constantly afraid. Wherefrom does this fear come? Is it our nature? Our nature is fearlessness, why bring into it something that is foreign? Vedanta tells us: Shake off all weakness, all fear. A child of God should not be afraid of anything. If you want to rise, make yourself strong. But you must do it for yourself and you can only do it by right thinking.

The mind is the instrument by which we accomplish everything. Our mind thinks—that thought creates, and what it creates we see in the external activity of our life. So we must train this mind. We must not let it run wild. We must curb it and use discrimination. The world approaches us under two forms, one is good and the other pleasant. One appeals to our physical nature and the other to our deeper nature; but that deeper nature is not awake in all. There are some who almost forget that they possess a higher nature or that they have any connection with the Supreme. Yet the higher nature is there, latent within their heart; and when they appeal to that nature and try to judge everything through the light of that higher nature, it is gradually awakened and all their activity becomes directed by it. Then they cannot go astray, they cannot do anything wrong.

As we unfold our spiritual consciousness, we think and live aright. Whatever approaches us we take at its proper valuation and not as it appears. Nothing can deceive us; therefore we do not labor for what is false and unreal. There are people who work faithfully, but they feel the burden of life because their effort does not bring the desired results. Why is this? It is because their effort is not controlled by discrimination; it is not directed by a purpose that is definite and single. Single-heartedness does not come until we have the higher faculty of discrimination awakened within us. Only then do we think consciously and we are not led away by passing fancies. If something arises that appeals to us and arouses our desire, we do not struggle to gain it without reflecting whether it will bring us a blessing or not.

Human beings should not run after shadows. We are superior to animals in just this, that we have the power to discriminate; and only as we use it, shall we learn the secret of right thinking and right living. When our thoughts are free from impurity and self-consciousness, our light will shine. But how often we forget this and try to gain our selfish ends, even by unworthy means. We believe too much in things which are temporary and neglect that which is lasting. When, however, our thoughts become connected with our inner nature, then not only will the light shine in the spiritual realm which now seems dark to us, but our life here will also be filled with clearness, directness and fearlessness.

The religious life does not mean devoting certain hours to the study of the Bible or some other sacred Scripture; it means continuous life in accordance with the higher law. And nowhere do we find this more strikingly illustrated than in the Hindu life. It is said that the Hindus eat religion, drink religion, sleep religion. What is the significance of this? That they do not wish to live without God; that they do not want to be separated for one moment from that supreme consciousness. They believe that all their actions, from the least important to the loftiest, must start from that one central consciousness. This is what we need to learn, —that at all times we must lead exalted lives, that every act must be in harmony with our higher nature, that we must serve our Ideal even at the cost of our life. Such characters are needed, and we can build them only by right thinking.

We must not shut ourselves up in one set of doctrines and dogmas and believe that the whole spiritual Truth is confined in them. According to Vedanta, Truth is the common property of the whole human race; and whoever is wakeful, whoever applies the Truth, whoever lives the life, he is a follower of the Truth, whether he comes from East or West. A flower is a flower wherever it grows, and it gives the same fragrance to the one who tramples on it as to the one who cherishes it. That is the nature we should develop. We must not say: This person does not appeal to me; I cannot love or serve him. The ordinary man does that. The flower does not refuse its fragrance to any one; it gives what it has to give. Similarly our higher nature should be so unfolded that we can feel for all and give without asking anything.

When that comes, we can truly be

called children of God. Then our religion will not be merely a matter of creed or Scripture, it will be a reality; and this reality is religion. Religion is based on realization. Unless it has become real to us, no amount of argument or reasoning, no amount of observance of outer forms, can bring us anything. We must live the life without condemnation or denunciation. We must let our soul manifest in us. If we have an ideal, we must let it grow; and as it grows it will produce its own effect. What we need therefore is to cultivate our spiritual nature and we do this by right thought. It does not matter what others may think. There is no reason why we should not think in the right way, for what we think, that we reflect. If we have love in our hearts, we send out into the universe a current of love which is united with a similar current; but if we hold unworthy, hateful thoughts, they will come back to us. We shall create conditions which will be hateful to us and which will set in motion forces which we shall afterwards regret, but which we shall not be able to resist. We can avoid this only by thinking from the beginning in the right way.

Our thought is the seed which determines the fruit of our action. If the seed is good, then the flowers and fruit which come from the seed must be good and must prove beneficial to ourselves and others. But if we plant in our hearts a poisonous seed, it will harm not only ourselves but all who come in contact with us. Human life is a great responsibility. Only a thoughtless man will say: I cannot help what happens, I am not responsible. We are constantly influencing ourselves and our fellow-beings by what we think, because our thought shapes our inner nature and we radiate consciously or unconsciously what we are. Let us be wakeful then. Let us be thoughtful in whatever we do. Let us be faithful to our true Self; for all blessings must come to us, if we prove ourselves true to our higher nature.

V.

THE VALUE OF NON-ATTACHMENT

The real treasure is that laid up through charity and piety, temperance and self-control. The treasure thus hid is secure, and passes not away.—*Teachings of Buddha.*

It is the business of a musician to harmonize every instrument, but of a well-educated man to adapt himself harmoniously to every fortune.—*Demophilus the Pythagorean.*

As the strength of the tree shows itself in the fruit, so the true divine strength in a man is shown in his good works and virtues. "There is no faith without works."—*Jacob Boehme.*

SERENITY of heart is attained when all the blemishes are wiped out of our nature through the subjugation of self. Only when we have succeeded in eliminating all worldly impressions and we no longer allow our mind to cling to the non-essential, can we attain perfect tranquillity; and we do this through the practice of non-attachment. For this reason non-attachment forms one of the most vital factors in our spiritual path. In order to gain it people subject themselves to rigid austerities and sacrifices. But these do not always lead to detachment. Often we find as much attachment in a beggar as in a prince. It is not a question of many possessions or few. Non-attachment is a quality of mind and has very little to do with external conditions. Through a momentary impulse due to unhappy circumstances we may tear ourselves away from our association and environment; but even by doing this, we are not able to break the tie which binds us to them. The outer renunciation of earthly things does not liberate us from the hold they have upon our mind.

We usually imagine that we feel attachment only for what is pleasing to us, but in reality aversion binds us as much as desire. It is sometimes even more difficult to free ourselves from unpleasant impressions than from pleasant ones. There are certain blunders, hasty words, unworthy acts, which leave a bad taste in our memory and we would like to forget them; but we seem powerless to do so, because our mind stubbornly clings to them. Often, too, we recognize something plainly detrimental to our progress, yet we are unable to drive it out of our thought.

Another mistake we frequently make is to suppose that there cannot be any true love without strong attachment. In reality, however, they are totally different in nature and produce contrary results on our character. Attachment contracts, love expands. Attachment calls out all the baser selfish instincts. We are attached because of the gratification it brings us, with only a secondary thought for the happiness and well-being of the one to whom we are attached. Love, on the other hand, makes us absolutely forgetful of our own self-interest or satisfaction and mindful only of the loved one. It gives perfect freedom, while attachment creates slavery both for us and for the one towards whom we bear attachment. Love gives for the joy of giving, attachment gives for the return that may come.

Those who have a perfect understanding of the spiritual life declare that attachment in any form is a great drawback; and if we wish to advance on the spiritual path, we must practise non-attachment towards all these world impressions, associations and possessions to which we cling at present through sheer force of habit. By this, however, is meant an inner practice rather than an outer act of renunciation. It is a question of creating new impressions in the mind. If our present impressions have proved unsatisfactory and hostile to our progress, then we must take a stand against them.

We do this and no more. We must not fight them, but we must go to work and create a totally new set of impressions.

The ego is our greatest enemy in accomplishing this. It constantly produces delusion in our mind. Yet if it is helpful to us, we do not wish to destroy it. What we want is to reshape it. We want a better form of ego. This is the idea of all discipline. The only way we can conquer this subtle force is to hold ourselves as the witness. As we would stand on the bank of a river and see the water flow by, so we should watch all impressions pass without being disturbed by them. The ordinary tendency is, when some one strikes, to strike back; but this is not the case with a man of masterful mind. It is not that he lacks in sensibility, but these things do not move him; he has, as it were, put on an armour of fortitude and calmness.

The practice of detachment includes two distinct processes,—withdrawing and indrawing. We must withdraw ourselves from whatever retards our unfoldment; then create a strong new spiritual impression by turning our thought within. At present we are all slaves to certain habits; in order to overcome these we must cultivate other habits, which in time will become so dominant that they will efface the old ones. All our out-going tendencies, which now hold us back, must be detached from the non-essential and then drawn inward. But this is only possible through superior knowledge.

If we try to do violence to our mind by a sudden uprooting of the old impressions, it suffers; but if we first acquire a correct knowledge of the relative value of things, the mind itself lets go without any pang. First we analyze, discriminate and try to see everything in its true light;

then as the mind gradually detaches itself from the old impression, we turn it inward and fix it on some spiritual object. As we do this, our heart becomes more and more liberated from the non-essential and finds its sole delight in God.

VI.

WORK AND RENUNCIATION

Give up everything to Him, resign yourself to Him and there will be no more trouble for you. Then you will come to know that everything is done by His will. To live in the world or to leave it depends upon the will of God. Therefore, work, leaving everything to Him. What else can you do?—*Sri Ramakrishna.*

To work alone thou hast the right, but never to the fruits thereof. Be thou neither actuated by the fruits of action, nor be thou attached to inaction.—*Bhagavad-Gita.*

WHEN we have reached God-knowledge, bondage drops from us just as ripe fruit drops from the tree. But if we tear the fruit from the tree, it does not ripen. In the same way when our desires are unfulfilled within us, if we merely tear them out of our heart, the heart bleeds. Renunciation is never possible in that way. As our understanding unfolds, however, and we outgrow the little things of this world, just as children outgrow their toys, our desires drop off of their own accord; it requires no tearing, no pain, no pang. Spiritual unfoldment must always take place gradually. We cannot force it. The first step in the practice of renunciation is to learn to work without selfish attachment. "Renunciation and performance of action both lead to liberation," Sri Krishna says in the Gita. "Children (the ignorant) alone say, not wise men, that the path of wisdom and the path of work are different. He who is truly established in one obtains the fruits of both."

One who is a true worker attains that highest ideal which is reached by a man of renunciation. Work is not a hindrance to spiritual growth, as some imagine; we are all working constantly. There is a pent-up energy within each one of us which must find expression. If we do not know how to direct it properly, we create more and more bondage for ourselves;

but if we understand how to use it, then every act liberates us and creates more wisdom, more strength and illumination.

We must follow the path of action so long as we have to struggle to subdue ourselves; when everything within has become tranquil, then we can take up the life of contemplation. First is the battle, then the calm. We must all fight against the various forces which are trying to overthrow us. Again and again desire rises like a storm and shakes our whole being; only when it is conquered can we gain the state of meditation necessary to attain wisdom.

Our ignorance lasts so long as we confine ourselves to our lower nature and identify ourselves wholly with it. But when we acquire knowledge of That which is unbounded, unlimited, perfect, then we naturally overcome all imperfections and the petty little tendencies which create bondage fall away from us. It is the little man who becomes jealous of another, envious of another, who tries to further his own interest by hurting another. As he grows bigger in spiritual wisdom his nature unfolds, his consciousness expands, until the whole universe becomes his abode and all mankind his family. This is what is meant by renunciation. It does not mean giving up external things; it means giving up limitation and allowing the soul to expand its circle. We do not drop anything, we merely live and act in a greater circle. We breathe more freely, enjoy more freely, give more freely.

He who has conquered his lower self by his higher Self is always self-controlled and serene-minded, for his higher Self is never affected by the dualities. It is the same in pleasure or pain, in honor or dishonor; it remains ever tranquil and unmoved. Such a man has attained freedom. Nothing can overthrow him. Freedom, however, is not license. We are free when nothing can strike us down; when our whole nature is under our control; when we are the master of body, senses, mind and will; when we know that we are the changeless Self. He whose heart is filled with this knowledge of Spirit has equal regard for friends and foes, for well-wishers and ill-wishers, for the righteous and the unrighteous. How then can he hate any creature, how can he shrink from any one, when to him all is One Supreme Reality? This is the basis of the brotherhood of man which Christ teaches; by this realization alone can we connect ourselves with all men.

No matter what our line of activity is, we must hold to this thread and follow it; for if we miss that, then we have nothing to support us. The path of wisdom, of work, of devotion, of meditation, the ultimate goal of all these is but one and that one is the Supreme Lord Who exists everywhere. He is in our work and He is also in our rest. He dwells in every heart. He is outside as well as within. When we realize Him, then this world can deceive us no more, for we feel ourselves connected with Him in Whom everything exists and finding Whom we can lose nothing.

VII.

THE SPIRIT OF CONSECRATION

Whatever thou doest, whatever thou eatest, whatever thou offerest as oblation, whatever thou givest and the austerities thou performest, do that as an offering to Me. Thus thou shalt be freed from the bonds of action.—*Bhagavad-Gita.*

He whose works proceed from himself, does little good service to God; while he who suffers himself to be guided by the Holy Spirit, does great works even in small actions.—*John Tauler.*

WITHOUT a spirit of consecration our life must invariably remain unproductive. It is not that we do not work or that we do not try to do good, but we miss our aim; because all our thoughts and actions, to bear real fruit, must be backed by something higher than our physical self. For that reason wise men have the habit of consecrating themselves in all that they undertake. There are two ways of doing everything—one, with small personal ends in view; the other, with the larger end of universal good. Each thing done can be consecrated or desecrated. A selfish aim will desecrate even the finest act. We see therefore that all this field of work provided for our development is in itself neither good nor bad. It is good, if it leads us towards our object; it is bad, if it makes us miss our goal. We cannot keep on revolving with the wheel of life aimlessly. We must learn to follow our higher instincts and not be distracted by the voices of the world. We must cultivate a true spirit of consecration.

This world would be a very different place if we would all live up to our Ideal; for when we form the habit of consecrating ourselves in every thought and action, an exalted atmosphere of selfless love is created, which surrounds us wherever we go. All the unrest of the heart ceases when our Ideal completely fills our life;

because no room is left for small trivial concerns. Therefore the wise ones, instead of making a fixed set of rules for us, merely ask us to offer everything to the Lord. When we give ourselves wholly to God and make Him our constant aim, we do not need any special exercises. The only thing needful is to start with some lofty thought and think it again and again, until finally we move and have our being in that one thought. This is what is called having an Ideal.

If we learn to live our life with a genuine sense of consecration, we find it unnecessary to calculate and plan; because our individual will works naturally in unity with the universal Will and we move in perfect harmony with the great cosmic plan. It is always dangerous when we rely on our little ego. We must learn to walk with God and depend on Him alone. When we learn this, we may go on doing what we are doing now, but we shall do it with consecration. Although our hands and feet, our senses and mind will continue to be active, they will work with a new purpose, because they are consciously connected with the Source.

At present we may not have a taste for spiritual things, because we have formed the habit of longing for the things of this world; so spiritual things are not pleasing to us. But we must try to cultivate another taste. As we have formed the habit of worldly desires, so we should form a new spiritual habit. We have lived so long in close contact with the physical world that it alone seems real and important, while the spiritual world is vague and unimportant to us. But if we will try to know more of that unfamiliar realm, we shall begin to feel its reality and our life will be transformed. Then when misfortune or even death overtakes us, we shall not be overwhelmed or forget our Ideal.

This is the purpose of all spiritual practice—to fortify us against the moments of trial and enable us to stand firmly, so that we may not lose our higher point of view and turn aside from the path. When we are able to make God a living Presence in our life, then His light will shed its radiance even in the hours of darkness and sadness. This living consciousness of the Presence, however, cannot be forced. The veil must drop from our mind. We must not allow ourselves to be intoxicated by unwholesome influences of the world, but we must open ourselves wholly to the more powerful influence of God. Nothing helps us to do this so much as the spirit of consecration. But we should never talk of it. It is something to be expressed silently, as the flower opens in silence and unperceived; but that silent, enduring service to God will generate a power more potent than any material force we know.

Let us humbly seek our Ideal and serve Him in every thought, word and action. We cannot form an absolute Ideal with the finite mind; but our Ideal will grow and gradually become vast and all-embracing, as the unbounded Deity within us is able to manifest more and more of His greatness. When He fills our whole heart, all pettiness and ignorance and self-seeking will vanish; and instead of thinking ourselves great through self-importance, we shall feel ourselves great only in Him. Let us never forget that without His strength we are weak, without His support we are sure to stumble; but that if we will turn to Him whenever we have need of help, He will never fail to lead us out of the darkness and fill our groping mind with the light of understanding.

The sooner we turn to God, the better it will be for us; because as we delay, we retard our evolution and growth. He is the very essence of our being, our only Resting-place, our one safe Guide and Protector. When we realize this and offer ourselves in complete surrender at His feet, then will He take our life, bless it, consecrate it and fill it full of divine beauty and holiness.